First Published in the
United States of America, November 2017

Gingko Press, Inc.
1321 Fifth Street
Berkeley, CA 94710, USA
www.gingkopress.com
ISBN 978-1-58423-678-8

Published under license from Graffito Books Ltd
www.graffitobooks.com
©(text and images) Zebedee Helm 2017

Printed in China

I don't think much of this one

I like the yellow

Kit & Willy's

GUiDE TO....

ART

whoops!

definitely NOT by Zebedee Helm

GiNGKO PRess

the Introduction

me KIT

Cookie
(chocolate c

Hi,
I'm Kit and this is my dog, Willy.
We are full of something that my
parents call CURIOSITY. It
means that we are always putting
our noses into things and
INVESTIGATING (unless it's
KALE which we leave well alone).
I am a cowboy now, but when I
grow up I might be a
DETECTIVE or an ARTIST.

WILLY
a Dackish Dackish
Sausage dog

art
gallery

This week we went to an art gallery to investigate ART. If you
want to understand art, you have to ask QUESTIONS. Grown-ups
always give you answers, as long as you ask POLITELY.

Important advice....

When you visit the art gallery, as well as a pad of paper and a holster full of pencils, go in your SOCKS. The floors in art galleries are very polished, in fact they are normally SO shiny that you can SLIDE all the way from one room into the next one. SLIDE over the page to learn EVERYTHING about ART...

⟶

OLD Portraits

silly hat

big
nose

distinguish
expressic

fancy
patterns

NTOINE PARIS Consc
Etat né en 1668 mort e

These are normally VERY boring but occasionally you see a good one or rather a good one SEES YOU. This is because the eyes actually FOLLOW you around the room, no matter WHERE you are standing! Other non boring portraits are ones of particularly ugly people and those with funny things in the background, like monkeys, or weird looking dogs.

...If you want to paint a portrait then your model has to sit VERY still and to do this you need to give them lots of jazz music and sausages. If they don't sit still after ALL THAT, then take a photograph of them instead and go to the park with a frisbee.

Impressionism

umbrella

Lady

Water

lily pads

IMPRESSIONISM is quite easy to spot. It is always a painting and normally has a lady, some water, a boat, an umbrella, lily pads, and a tree in it. If you look at one VERY close up it is lots of different coloured dots and splodges of paint and you think that a baby might have done it.

...To be an Impressionist you have to work OUTSIDE, and you MUST have a BEARD and a HAT.

FAUVISM

Wild swimming

Wild colours

Wild Park keeper

The Fauvists were artists who valued COLOUR above ALL other things, EVEN CHOCOLATE! They saw the world in peculiar tones and that's exactly how they painted it. If you've got a BRAND NEW paint box then Fauvism is for YOU, but when you've messed it up, and got BLUE in the YELLOW, and GREEN in the PURPLE, then you'll have to move onto something else.

What you Will Probably Need...

...You will certainly and definitely need SUNGLASSES, as otherwise all those BRIGHT and CRAZY colours will leave you COMPLETELY dazzled.

Cubism

bit of guitar

NEWS

newspaper

another bit
of guitar

CUBISM was invented by some artists who were short of paper. They wanted to do lots of different pictures of the SAME thing but only had ONE piece of paper. There are always a lot of edges and not quite finished bits of guitar and a newspaper. The result is you look at it, you go CROSS-EYED and then your head starts hurting.

Remember...

...Try not to dream in cubism because the FLOOR will be on the CEILING, and your HEAD is where your BOTTOM should be, and you will NEVER be able to find your way back to bed to wake up.

De ~~Stijyl~~ Stijl

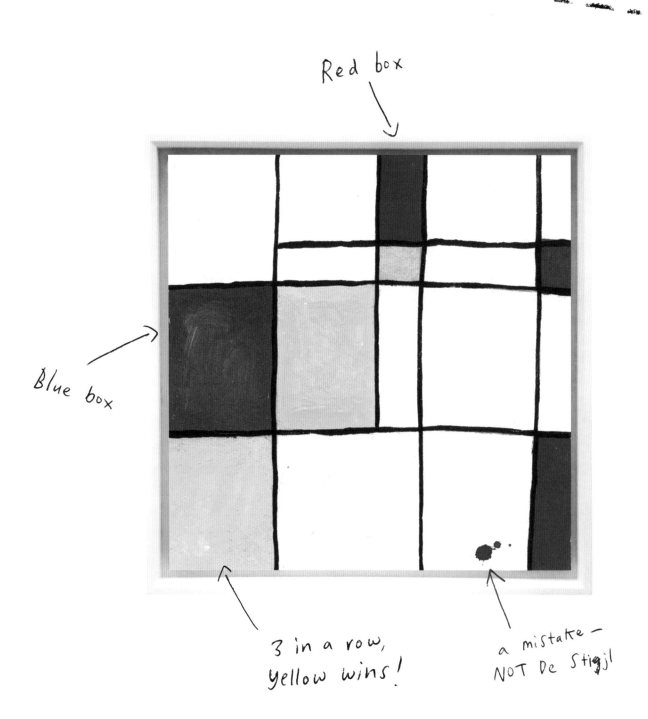

Red box

Blue box

3 in a row, yellow wins!

a mistake — NOT De Stijl

This art is difficult to pronounce and almost impossible to spell, but it is actually quite easy to do. It is basically red, blue and yellow boxes with some black lines. Not just paintings, but also buildings, clothes and not very comfy FURNITURE, can come in this ~~stijl~~ style.

You MUST Remember...

...With De Stijl you MUSTN'T do a painting that is actually OF anything. Your creation can ONLY be LINES and COLOURS, NOT interesting things, like SHARKS.

Surrealism

lobster

Jelly

Not a pipe

This normally has a pipe or a LOBSTER in it, so is actually quite easy to spot. You don't have to use paint to do Surrealism, you can use jelly or just stand on your head and bark like a dog. Simply make or do the most UNEXPECTED thing you can think of, and when people laugh, tell them it isn't funny, it is actually SURREALISM.

What you WILL need...

... A very long and twirly MOUSTACHE and to be able to pull funny faces when people take your photograph.

AbstRact EXPRessionism

feelings

Really strong feelings

If you aren't any good at drawing things to look like what they're supposed to then DON'T PANIC, you can just become an ABSTRACT EXPRESSIONIST. You can dribble paint all over the paper, the floor, your shoes ~~and even your dog~~, then tell everyone the picture represents how you feel.

What you ~~might~~ Will definitely Need...

...FEELINGS, lots of them, the more WILD and RUGGED the better. So, instead of having a fight with your dog or punching the wall, get your paints out and use them to show the world that you simply WILL NOT be eating KALE for supper, even if it IS good for you.

Pop Art

yellow
TERRIBLE spots, sh should wast more
Cambell's
KALE SOUP
OH BRAD! I'M SORRY BUT I CAN'T EVER LOVE A MAN WHO EATS KALE!!
YUK!!

Pop Art was done by artists who worked in their kitchens and liked comics. It is full of yellow, exclamation marks and EXPLOSIONS!! Other subjects for Pop Art are the things in your cupboard, like SOUP, and if you're not feeling hungry then you paint girls with very spotty faces and boyfriends called BRAD.

...Despite its name, Pop Art is NOT actually made out of things that GO POP, like balloons or bubble wrap, and it is DEFINITELY NOT made by gluing popcorn all over yourself, WILLY!

PERFORMANCE ART

ALWAYS wear black (or nothing)

1.

2.

important to keep a straight face

3.

BANG!

Unexpect

Meou

4.

This art is done by artists who enjoy showing off and acting, but aren't very good at either. Felt-tips, stone, rusty metal, coat hangers, wool and post-it notes don't provide enough possibilities for them to express their ideas, so they use their OWN BODIES (or someone else's) instead.

What You NEED...

...Unless you are mad, you WILL need an AUDIENCE. But DON'T let them clap, no matter how much they want to. If they want to show their appreciation, then they can give you lots of money from their credit cards, as they would with more traditional forms of art.

Land Art

Adorable little bird

Rocks doing Land Art

Rocks NOT doing Land Art

LiTTER, definitely NOT Land Art!

If you live outdoors, or get left behind after a family picnic, then this is the art for you. It is made from anything that nature has left lying around outside, normally rocks and leaves. If you get FED UP with trying to balance rocks on top of each other then you can make a huge pile of leaves, which as well as being LAND ART, is also useful for jumping into AND as a house for hedgehogs.

Important advice....

...If you have done some Land Art then you have to be prepared to say goodbye to it and leave it behind. Land Art ALWAYS looks better left where it was made and it hardly EVER fits in the car.

SCULPeTURES

Traditional sculpture found in towns of someone you've NEVER heard of. →

REAL pigeon (not part of the sculpture)

Summer isn't the best time for butter sculpture →

Most types of art can appear as sculptures - normally they are made from stone, wood or metal, but actually you CAN use ANYTHING you want, even BUTTER! Artists who make sculptures usually have BIG hands and quite SAUSAGEY fingers, and they simply CAN'T be dealing with fiddly little things like paintbrushes or pencils.

WHAT You will DEFINITLY need...

...A hot BATH, as sculptors are ALWAYS covered in DUST.

Conceptual Art

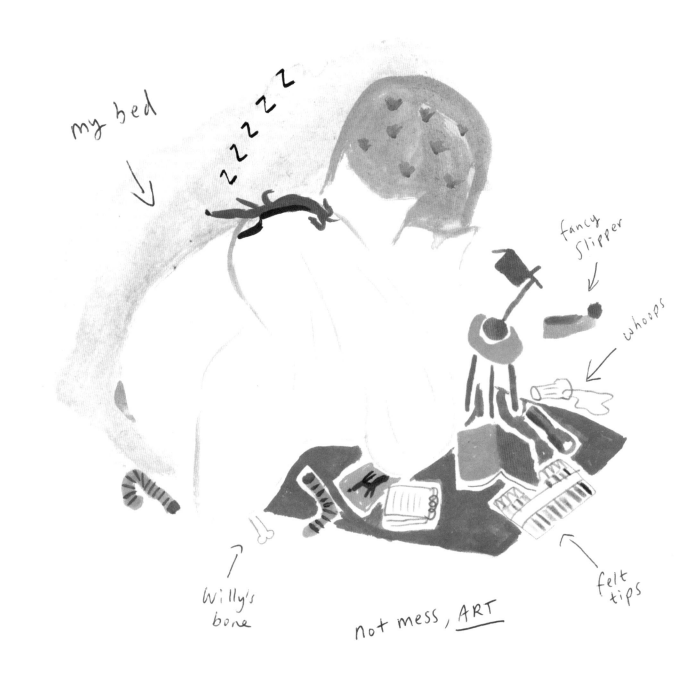

my bed

zzzz

fancy slipper

whoops

Willy's bone

not mess, ART

felt tips

This is what artists do when they've used up all the other styles. Things become art that weren't art, until you say they are. It's VERY useful if you get shouted at for not making your bed, or for leaving Lego all over the stairs. You just say "BUT IT'S CONCEPTUAL ART", and then you can look superior and misunderstood while sitting on the naughty step.

IMPORTANT advice...

...It's actually best to wait until you're GROWN UP to do your own CONCEPTUAL ART. It's just TOO similar to being naughty to get away with it.

STREET Art

Street
Art

Wall

Uninspired

Chewing
gum

If you have **LOTS** of paint but **NO** paper and live in a really boring
street that could do with some cheering up, then just go outside and
do some **STREET ART!** People who can't think of anything to
draw just write their names, but if you try hard you can come up
with something **REALLY** interesting that will bring the **WHOLE**
neighbourhood together for a chat.

...A ladder, a pair of fast shoes, a false name and a **VERY** good lawyer.

BUTTERFLY PRINTS

Exceptional handsomness →

But a bit pig-like because of the 2 noses →

↑
Fold here

These are created by painting something like a blob, or a brilliant self-portrait, on one side of the paper and then quickly folding it in half, pressing firmly with your hand, before unfolding, revealing a perfect MIRROR IMAGE! It will be no surprise to learn that this is one of the most popular art movements in the WHOLE wide world.

REMEMBER...

...MACARONI and other pasta shapes, sprayed GOLD and then stuck around your print make the most EXQUISITE frames, and truly complete your MASTERPIECE.

the Endroduction

It is important at the end of a trip round an art gallery to go to the café and RELAX. Understanding art makes it EVEN more INTERESTING, but it can make you VERY hungry too.

What we have learnt...

GENIUS!

← Chocolate mousse

... Looking at art by FAMOUS artists is FUN, But best of all is doing your own. And, no matter HOW limited your talents are, there is always SOMEONE who will appreciate that you are in fact a GENIUS.

Now please ~~exit~~ EXiT
through the
GiFT SHOP